Hal Leonard Student Piano Library

Piano Solos

Book 3
Revised Edition

Authors
**Barbara Kreader, Fred Kern,
Phillip Keveren, Mona Rejino**

Consultants
Tony Caramia, Bruce Berr,
Richard Rejino

Illustrator
Fred Bell

FOREWORD

Piano Solos presents challenging original music that coordinates page-by-page with the **Piano Lessons** book in the **Hal Leonard Student Piano Library**. The outstanding variety of composers and musical styles makes every solo an important piece in its own right – exciting to both performer and listener. In addition, each piece is designed to encourage and ensure further mastery of the concepts and skills in the **Piano Lessons** books.

May these **Piano Solos** become favorite pieces that delight all who hear and play them.

Best wishes,

Barbara Kreader
Phillip Keveren
Fred Kern
Mona Rejino

ISBN 978-0-7935-6272-5

Visit Hal Leonard Online at
www.halleonard.com

World headquarters, contact:
Hal Leonard
7777 West Bluemound Road
Milwaukee, WI 53213
Email: info@halleonard.com

In Europe, contact:
Hal Leonard Europe Limited
Dettingen Way
Bury St Edmunds, Suffolk, IP33 3YB
Email: info@halleonardeurope.com

In Australia, contact:
Hal Leonard Australia Pty. Ltd.
4 Lentara Court
Cheltenham, Victoria, 3192 Australia
Email: info@halleonard.com.au

Piano Solos Book 3

CONTENTS

✔ (at top of checklist column)

* Students can check pieces as they play them.

Racing Toward Home

Frantic (♩ = 112)

Katherine Beard

New Note–C

Blues Prelude

Slow Blues (♩ = 60)

Bill Boyd

mp

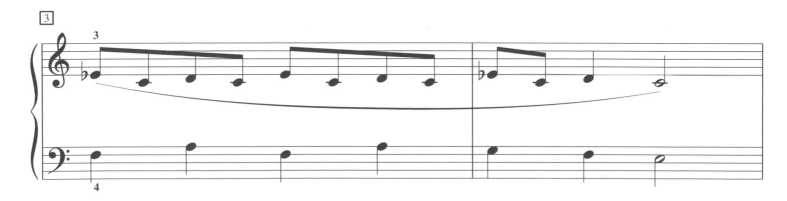

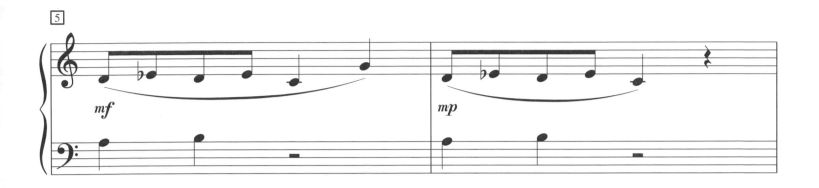

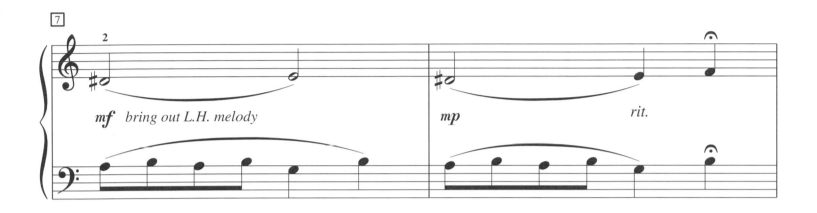

*A tempo means to return to the original tempo.

Hold pedal down

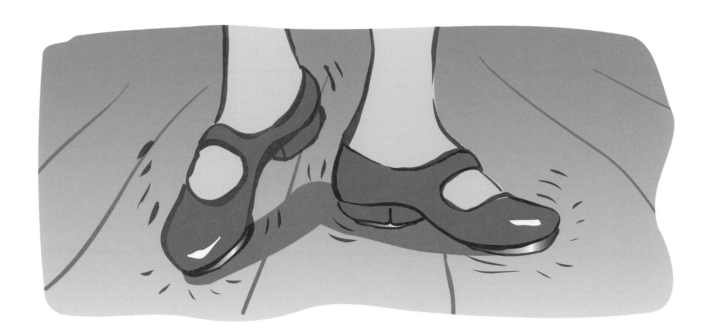

Tap Dance

With a lilt (swing eighth notes)

Bill Boyd

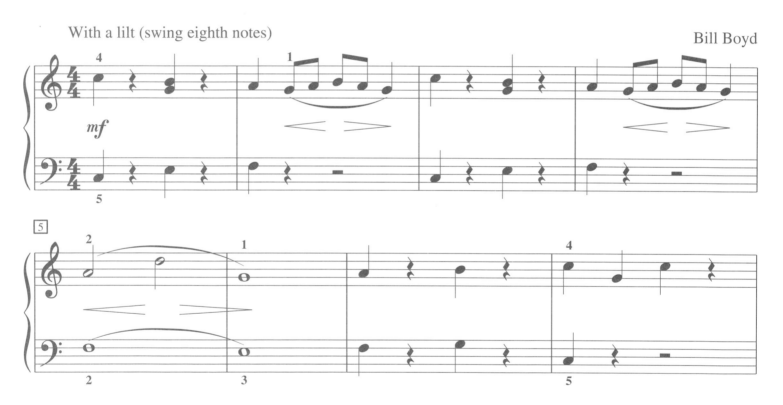

Accompaniment (Student plays one octave higher than written.)

With a lilt (♫ = ♪ ♪)(♩ = 145)

Tap on top of the piano or lap with both hands.

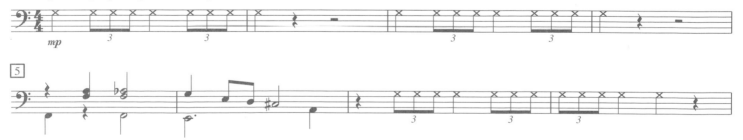

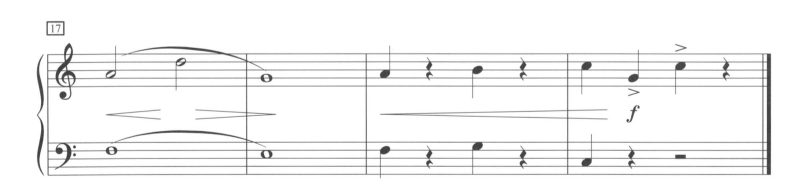

Fiesta March

Lively, but in strict rhythm (♩ = 155)

Bruce Berr

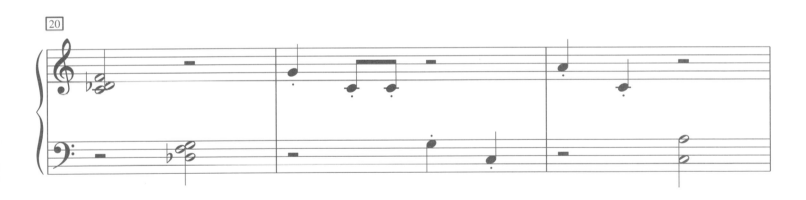

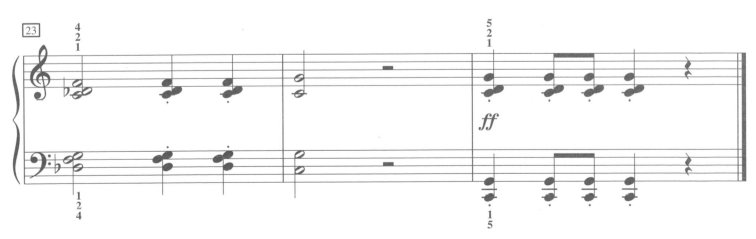

9

Leap Frog

Allegro jumpinoso (♩ = 155)

Carol Klose

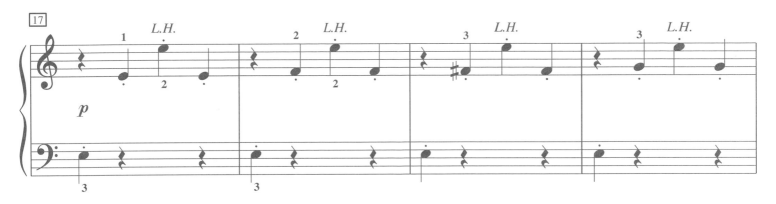

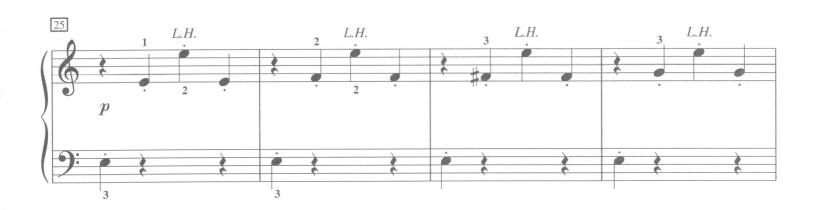

D.C. al Fine

Awesome Adventure

With power! ($\quad$ = 160)

Phillip Keveren

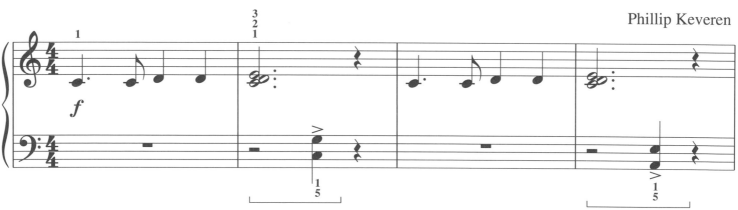

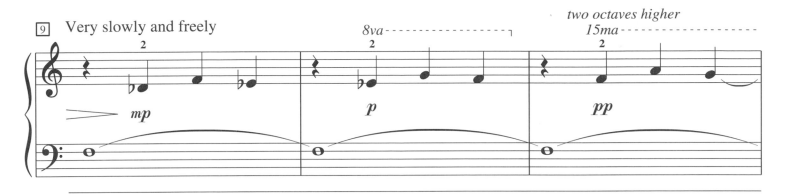

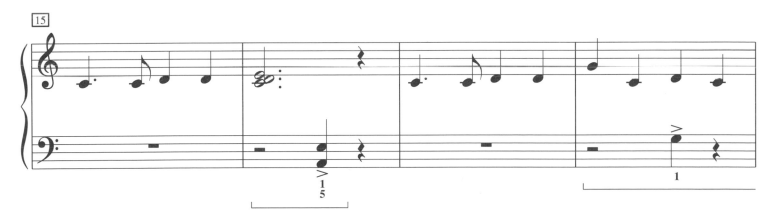

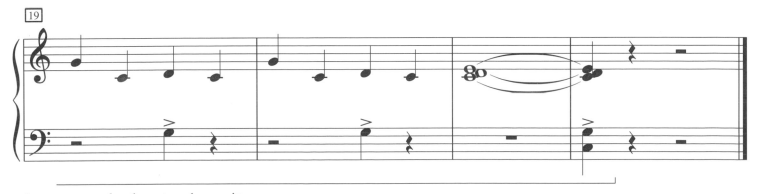

loco means to play the notes where written

B.B.'s Boogie

Bill Boyd

Lullaby Angel

for Lindsay Kay

Phillip Keveren

Flowing (♩ = 140)

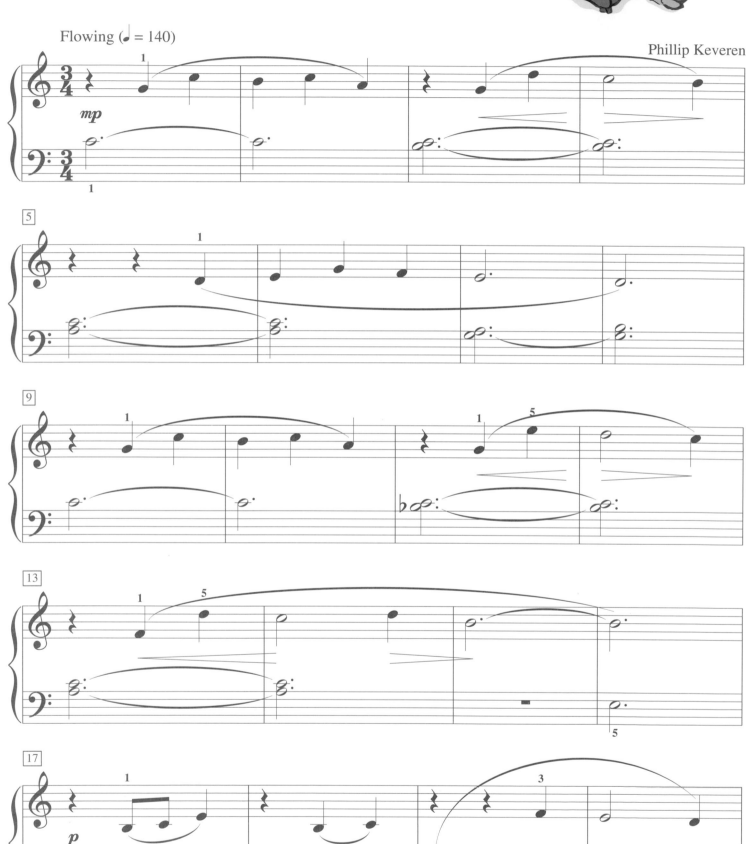

Hold down damper pedal to end.

The Banjo Picker

Allegro, with a steady beat (♩ = 192)

Carol Klose

The Clockwork Ballerina

Playfully (♩ = 120)

Christos Tsitsaros

The Winter Wind

Swirling fast (♩ = 192)

Carol Klose

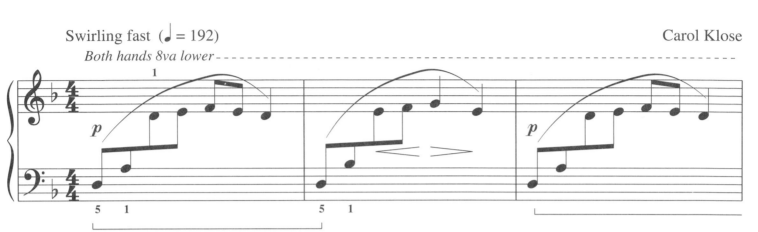

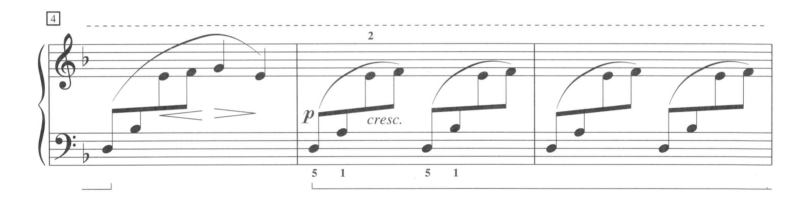

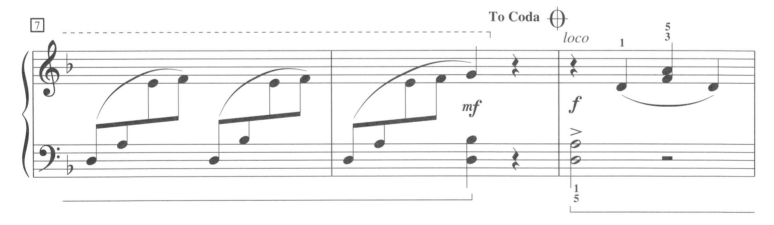

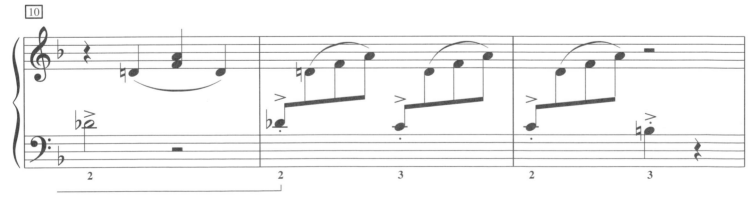

I Remember...

Slowly, from the heart (♩ = 96)

Phillip Keveren

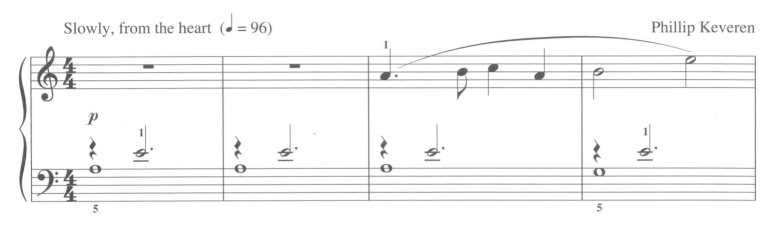

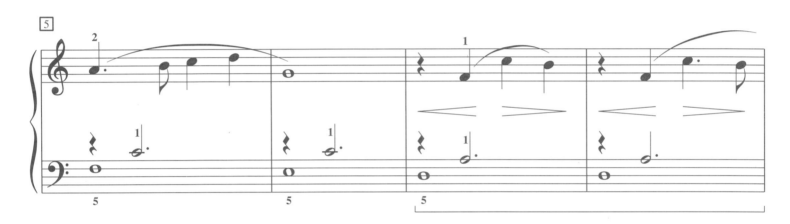

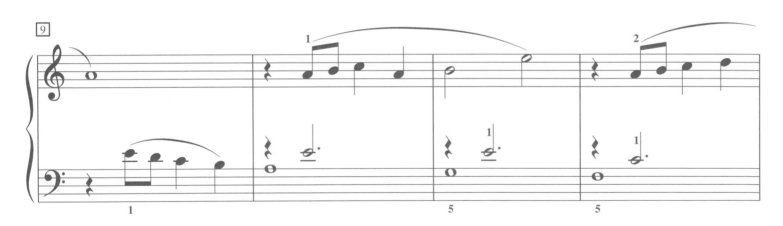

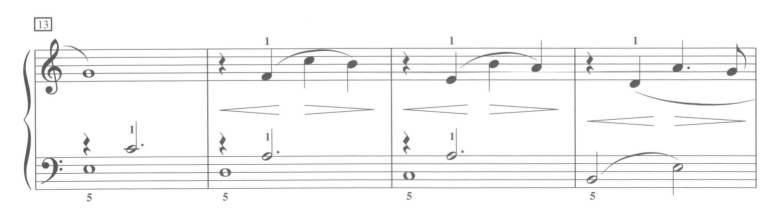

Use with Lesson Book 3, pg. 48

24

Baroque Boogie

for Sean David

Boogie! (swing eighth notes) (♩ = 140)

Phillip Keveren

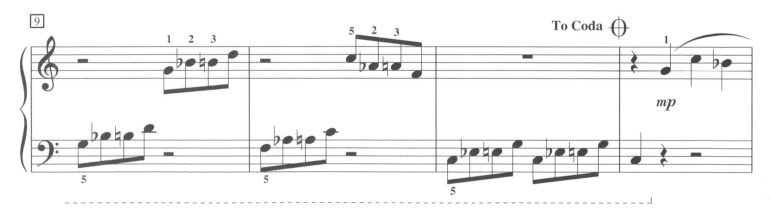

Properly (even eighth notes)

loco

D.C. al Coda

8va - - - - - - - - - - -

CODA

15ma - - - - - - - - - -
two octaves lower

27

Porcupine Pizzicato

Phillip Keveren

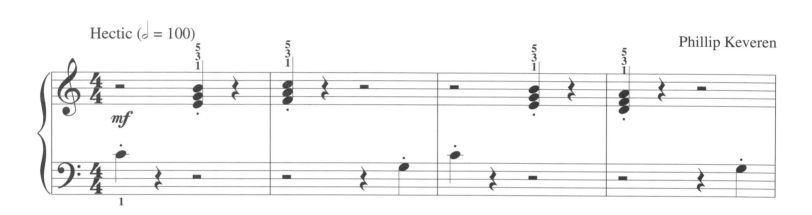

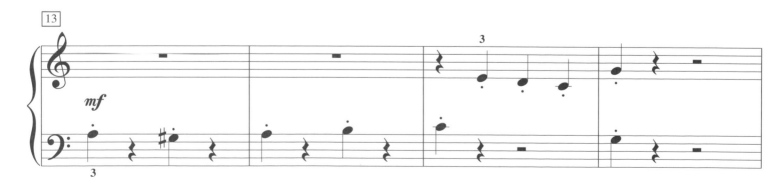

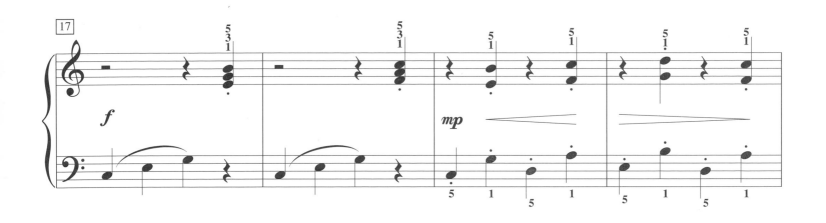

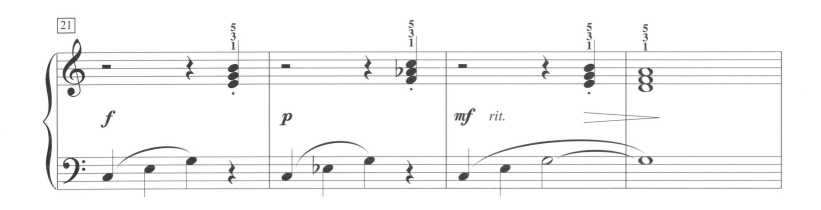

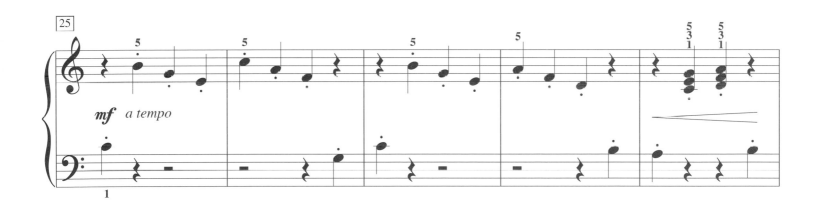

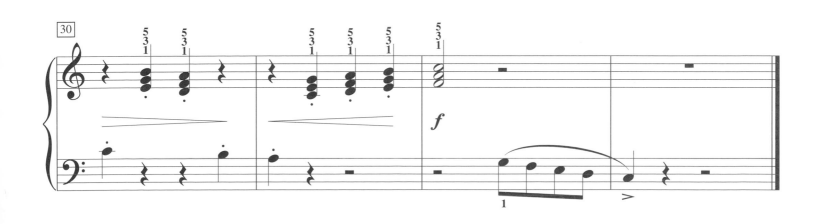

Gestures

Spirited (♩ = 180)

Fred Kern

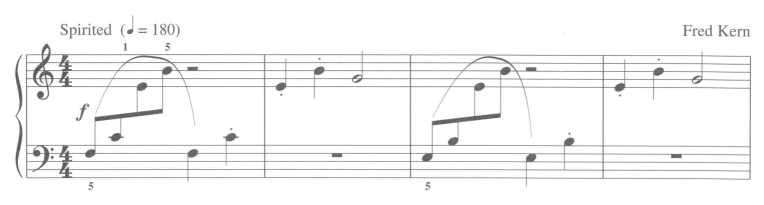

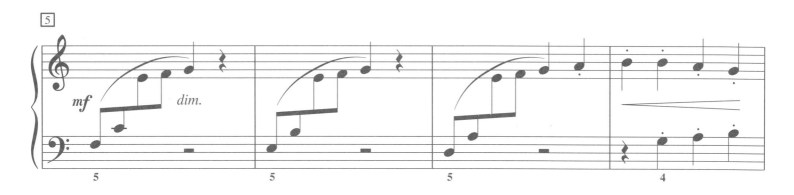

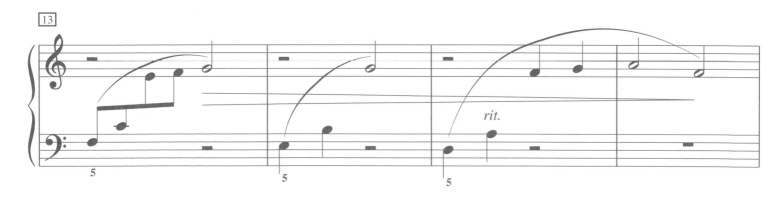

31

POPULAR SONGS
HAL LEONARD STUDENT PIANO LIBRARY

The **Hal Leonard Student Piano Library** has great songs, and you will find all your favorites here: Disney classics, Broadway and movie favorites, and today's top hits. These graded collections are skillfully and imaginatively arranged for students and pianists at every level, from elementary solos with teacher accompaniments to sophisticated piano solos for the advancing pianist.

Adele
arr. Mona Rejino
Correlates with HLSPL Level 5
00159590.....................$12.99

The Beatles
arr. Eugénie Rocherolle
Correlates with HLSPL Level 5
00296649.....................$12.99

Irving Berlin Piano Duos
arr. Don Heitler and Jim Lyke
Correlates with HLSPL Level 5
00296838.....................$14.99

Broadway Favorites
arr. Phillip Keveren
Correlates with HLSPL Level 4
00279192.....................$12.99

Chart Hits
arr. Mona Rejino
Correlates with HLSPL Level 5
00296710.......................$8.99

Christmas at the Piano
arr. Lynda Lybeck-Robinson
Correlates with HLSPL Level 4
00298194.....................$12.99

Christmas Cheer
arr. Phillip Keveren
Correlates with HLSPL Level 4
00296616.......................$8.99

Classic Christmas Favorites
arr. Jennifer & Mike Watts
Correlates with HLSPL Level 5
00129582.......................$9.99

Christmas Time Is Here
arr. Eugénie Rocherolle
Correlates with HLSPL Level 5
00296614.......................$8.99

Classic Joplin Rags
arr. Fred Kern
Correlates with HLSPL Level 5
00296743.......................$9.99

Classical Pop – Lady Gaga Fugue & Other Pop Hits
arr. Giovanni Dettori
Correlates with HLSPL Level 5
00296921.....................$12.99

Contemporary Movie Hits
arr. by Carol Klose, Jennifer Linn and Wendy Stevens
Correlates with HLSPL Level 5
00296780.......................$8.99

Contemporary Pop Hits
arr. Wendy Stevens
Correlates with HLSPL Level 3
00296836.......................$8.99

Cool Pop
arr. Mona Rejino
Correlates with HLSPL Level 5
00360103.....................$12.99

Country Favorites
arr. Mona Rejino
Correlates with HLSPL Level 5
00296861.......................$9.99

Disney Favorites
arr. Phillip Keveren
Correlates with HLSPL Levels 3/4
00296647.....................$10.99

Disney Film Favorites
arr. Mona Rejino
Correlates with HLSPL Level 5
00296809 ....$10.99

Disney Piano Duets
arr. Jennifer & Mike Watts
Correlates with HLSPL Level 5
00113759.....................$13.99

Double Agent! Piano Duets
arr. Jeremy Siskind
Correlates with HLSPL Level 5
00121595.....................$12.99

Easy Christmas Duets
arr. Mona Rejino & Phillip Keveren
Correlates with HLSPL Levels 3/4
00237139.......................$9.99

Easy Disney Duets
arr. Jennifer and Mike Watts
Correlates with HLSPL Level 4
00243727.....................$12.99

Four Hands on Broadway
arr. Fred Kern
Correlates with HLSPL Level 5
00146177.....................$12.99

Frozen Piano Duets
arr. Mona Rejino
Correlates with HLSPL Levels 3/4
00144294.....................$12.99

Hip-Hop for Piano Solo
arr. Logan Evan Thomas
Correlates with HLSPL Level 5
00360950.....................$12.99

Jazz Hits for Piano Duet
arr. Jeremy Siskind
Correlates with HLSPL Level 5
00143248.....................$12.99

Elton John
arr. Carol Klose
Correlates with HLSPL Level 5
00296721.....................$10.99

Joplin Ragtime Duets
arr. Fred Kern
Correlates with HLSPL Level 5
00296771.......................$8.99

Movie Blockbusters
arr. Mona Rejino
Correlates with HLSPL Level 5
00232850.....................$10.99

The Nutcracker Suite
arr. Lynda Lybeck-Robinson
Correlates with HLSPL Levels 3/4
00147906.......................$8.99

Pop Hits for Piano Duet
arr. Jeremy Siskind
Correlates with HLSPL Level 5
00224734.....................$12.99

Sing to the King
arr. Phillip Keveren
Correlates with HLSPL Level 5
00296808.......................$8.99

Smash Hits
arr. Mona Rejino
Correlates with HLSPL Level 5
00284841.....................$10.99

Spooky Halloween Tunes
arr. Fred Kern
Correlates with HLSPL Levels 3/4
00121550.......................$9.99

Today's Hits
arr. Mona Rejino
Correlates with HLSPL Level 5
00296646.......................$9.99

Top Hits
arr. Jennifer and Mike Watts
Correlates with HLSPL Level 5
00296894.....................$10.99

Top Piano Ballads
arr. Jennifer Watts
Correlates with HLSPL Level 5
00197926.....................$10.99

Video Game Hits
arr. Mona Rejino
Correlates with HLSPL Level 4
00300310.....................$12.99

You Raise Me Up
arr. Deborah Brady
Correlates with HLSPL Level 2/3
00296576.....................$7.95

HAL•LEONARD®

7777 W. Bluemound Rd. P.O. Box 13819 Milwaukee, WI 53213

Visit our website at **www.halleonard.com**

Prices, contents and availability subject to change without notice. Prices may vary outside the U.S.